PLAYSCRIPT 58

'vagina rex and the gas oven'

jane arden

CALDER AND BOYARS · LONDON

First published in Great Britain 1971
by Calder & Boyars Ltd
18 Brewer Street London W1R 4AS

All performing rights in this play
are strictly reserved and application
for performances should be made to
CMA Ltd
22 Grafton Street London W1

No performance of the play may
be given unless a licence has been
obtained prior to rehearsal

ISBN 0 7145 0796 2 Cloth Edition
ISBN 0 7145 0797 0 Paper Edition

Printed by photo-lithography
and made in Great Britain at
The Pitman Press, Bath

INTRODUCTION

When this play was first produced in February 1969 its
thesis on female oppression caused a considerable uproar.

As one of the outcomes of the production 'The Observer'
carried a piece called 'Are Women Oppressed?' as though
there was still some doubt about the matter.

The evolving ot the Women's Liberation Movement
over the past two years seems to denounce the impression
given by some journalists that this theme of women's rage
was somehow special to the author's psyche.

Separating the inner world from the outer is a
technique used to wall people in their 'private neurosis'.
The growth of solidarity between women hopefully suggests
that this game of divide and rule is drawing to a close -
political and personal are beginning to cleave unto one
another and yesterday's 'deranged' females are emerging as
today's formidable radical leaders.

Jane Arden

VAGINA REX AND THE GAS OVEN

VAGINA REX AND THE GAS OVEN was first performed at Jim Haynes' Arts Laboratory, Drury Lane, London, in February, 1969, with the following cast:

THE WOMAN	Sheila Allen
THE MAN	Victor Spinetti
FURIES	Charlie, Peter, Gyp, Sophie, Joe, Ann, Sue, Franz, Angela, Vicki...and others who came and went

The video broadcast was by Hilary Rawling and Jane Arden
The music was by Shawn Phillips and The Djinn
The graphics were by Alan Aldridge

The play was produced by Jack Bond and Jack Henry Moore

The play was directed by Jack Bond

(A dark theatre.

When a third of the audience have settled into their
seats...

Radio crackle - the sound is adjusted and the voice of
a WOMAN is heard)

WOMAN. I know of nothing more humiliating, than the
beginnings of a girl child's existence - the sniggering
of uncles - and the resignation of aunts pointing to a
future of biological landscapes.

(The radio goes dead for a moment.

Sound of a police siren.

Heavy radio crackle which dies away)

At fifteen, the alternatives presented themselves -
fight - submit - or go mad. I made a compromise -
a dance contracted between these three that would keep
me occupied for the next twenty years - until history
turned up a better card - or I was certified insane.

(Other WOMEN's voices enter the broadcast - forming
a chorus)

When I was five years old, I asked myself - "why does
my uncle have his rice pudding served to him in the
big leather chair?" His burly weight leaned on my
life like a rape.

Had I seen something that revealed a twisted factor in

9

my own nature - or something common to my world of
women?

I could never choose sacrifice or submission because
it was incarnate in my being - I could never be
illuminated into self-realisation because I was
imprisoned in the shadow world of changelings -
children and slaves - caught in a static dimension.

(A faint spot lighting the corner of the stage revealing
a forty-year-old MAN wearing a dark neat suit, seated
cross-legged on a stool, half concealed in the shadows,
reading a newspaper. Radio volume increases)

We have no language. The words of women have yet to
be written.

Woman's use of speech amounts to an assenting silence
or an unheard shriek.

Centuries of oppression have made of us cowards and
defeatists.

Any woman who continues to capitulate - any woman
who has 'made' it in a man's world - will be guilty -
is from now on guilty of complicity and collaboration in
the perpetuation of the world-wide age-old female
ghetto.

Can anyone believe that the story of woman's oppression
was born of my private pathological fantasy?

Until very recently the black man was imprisoned in
his 'neurosis' - and it was only when this 'neurosis'
was investigated and found to be repeated in the
existence of every member of black society that the
individual was metamorphosed into a vital political
force.

You are an undeveloped country - passive, submissive,
raped by white colonialism.

What language will we use to describe the oppressed if
woman no longer embodies the masochistic role?

(The MAN on stage reading the newspaper looks up from time to time as though half listening to the broadcast. Further increase in volume)

We must destroy the language.

Bird-brained - tender, intuitive - garrulous - unreliable - disloyal and weak.

We must destroy the language.

Who are they - these illogical rulers of the kitchen?

Gossiping - dirty - incomplete - moon-crazed temptresses.

Frigid - earth-shackled - competitive mermaids.

Empty reflective angels of mercy. Dolls, cats, hens whores, slags and bitches.

Soulless mirrors and trembling virgins.

We must destroy the language.

These monstrous mother Goddesses. These evil arms and devouring breasts.

These washers of dirty linen who long to be dominated and suppressed.

Our capacity to think - except in the service of that, which we are dangerously deluded into supposing is our own self-interest - is desperately limited and shrouded in veils of mystification.

"My dear lady", they hint, "There is nothing accurate in what you have observed - it's all in your poor tormented psyche, come with me to our nice expanding mental hospitals, where we'll teach you, once again, that it's not history - but your head".

We must destroy the language.

Submissive means ill.

Feminine means submissive.

Before my curious eye could light upon this world, I was aware of this hump upon my back - I have examined it - and that has held up my journey - but while I was deciphering the hump - it seemed to me the pieces contained the story of the world.

(The MAN on stage gets up from his chair folding away his newspaper. He walks slowly across the stage to the radio speaker)

VOICE ON RADIO. We must bring together the political and the psychological. Radical action must liberate the whole being.

(The MAN kicks the speaker. The VOICE distorts)

... sub-culture of man.

(The MAN kicks the speaker again. It is silent. He stares at the audience - a tight smile on his lips)

MAN. Bloody lesbians! - bloody dykes! What they need is a good fuck!

(He sits down on his stool.

Lights up on MUSICAL GROUP seated front right of stage. Piano/Organ, guitar, drums. A young female singer, thin, witchlike, with a wailing reed-like voice, dressed in mythological costume.

From the shadows at the back of the stage a WOMAN emerges clutching a large teddy bear.

She is thirty-ish, a tall imposing creature with long flowing hair.

She is wearing loose black trousers, a white lace blouse and a black velvet jacket.

Her hair is tied back away from her face.

She minces childishly toward the group - a little party-girl.

Lights glow, coloured and fairylike casting large moving shadows - revealing the FURIES.

The FURIES - people of the streets - those who live faceless - exposed to violence - the homeless who haunt the wastelands of the world - telling us of our lost lives.

FURIES dancing as animated puppets - each one miming an individual doll - a nightmare nursery, illuminated by shafts of moonlight.

They are wearing old trousers and tee-shirts - their usual clothes.

Some should wear baggy white trousers (to pick up the ultra-violet lights later)

GROUP begin the song Dear Mary Grant in vaudevillian style.

The WOMAN and the FEMALE singer share the lyrics. The WOMAN speaks her lines. They coyly suggest in falsetto voices, the 'secret world' of little girls.

Bubble effects from the overhead projector)

WOMAN. (little girl voice)
    Dear Mary Grant.

SINGER. (little friend)
    Dear Mary Grant
    I'm very blue

WOMAN.
    My boyfriend's gone away.
    What shall I do?

SINGER.)
WOMAN.) (together)
>I told my friend
>and she agrees

WOMAN.
>He isn't <u>worth</u> - the tears I shed.
>He isn't <u>worth</u> the blinding pain -
>And I should <u>use</u> - my <u>brain.</u>

SINGER.)
WOMAN.) (together)
>But Mary Grant
>I try and try.

WOMAN.
>My brain won't work.
>I think I'll - <u>die</u>
>He's such a <u>lovely</u> boy
>And very <u>smart</u>

SINGER.
>D'you think I'm wrong?

WOMAN.
>D'you think I'm wrong?
>Dear Mary Grant...

SINGER.
>Dear Mary Grant...

WOMAN.
>To break my heart
>(Sighing)
>signed Blue eyes!

>(The theatre darkens.

>ONE of the FURIES steps forward to the edge of the stage.

>He stares stonily, aggressively into the audience)

14

FURY.
Women enjoy being dominated sexually.
Women enjoy being dominated sexually!
(Short silence)
Women enjoy being humiliated.
Women enjoy being humiliated.
(Short silence)
(Very aggressive)
The natural role for women is the submissive one!

(Sound of wind, sun and space.

FURIES gather into group as mediaeval worshippers
for sun-raising.

Projections on back of theatre of universe galaxy,
nebulae, the cosmos exploding stars. Overhead
projections (liquids, moire patterns), at least two
slide projectors and 16 m.m. movie.

General ultra-violet lighting.

The FURIES are now grouped together near the back
wall of the theatre. The tallest raises a large brilliant
symbol of the sun, painted in fluorescent colours. As
the symbol is slowly raised, the FURIES kneel and
stretch up their arms towards it in worship.

The sun is moved very slowly 180 degrees.

Tape - an electronic hum merging into wind.

During the sun raising - (on tape) - a disembodied
FEMALE VOICE in slowly celestial chanting tones)

VOICE.
The window is arranged
So that a hole
leads to the sun
the chimney pots are outside -
in my room.
Just the other side of the underneath,
I must keep my distance -
or the distance between us

16

we are spatially related
but fusion is not possible.
We come together
but are not one and the same
I am inviting you pot, into my room - with my eye
They have defined us clearly
you are a cracked pot
and I am a crackpot
the difference is marginal
but enough to keep us apart.

(The sound of ambulance sirens wailing.

Projection of ambulance head on.

FURIES move into a clinical block formation.

They stand poised in silent menace.

Projected HOSPITAL ATTENDANT pushing wheelchair.

The WOMAN walks on tiptoe - arms outstretched - on
an imaginary tightrope. She faces the audience and
staggers into a half-faint.

She is caught by one male FURY and lowered into the
arms of another.

Strobe lights flash on and off.

The FURIES spring individually out of their positions
and encircle the WOMAN, their silver claws extended.

One by one they scream and gesture at her.

The sound of violent electronic shorting.

The WOMAN convulses in the arms of two male
FURIES.

The WOMAN is laid prostrate on the floor.

One by one the FURIES circle around the WOMAN
trailing their claws across her face.

The strobe quickens. Deafening electronic feedback
from guitar and tape.

Violent, cathartic music from the GROUP.

The FURIES leap in frenzy over and around the
WOMAN.

The orgiastic strobe dance continues for some
minutes.

A FURY comes to the edge of the stage and stares into
the audience)

FURY. Women enjoy being dominated.

(GROUP sing a slow, thin, distant prophecy.

The FURIES sway - fragile - weed-like - frail as
fronds.

The voices of the GROUP echo - from the dead. There
is ectoplasm in the air.

Projections of X-rays)

GROUP.
Who are those figures in white?
Are they the angels of light?
Or are they spiders on the wall
About to fall on me?
Is that a table or a chair?
Is it there?
Or are they atoms whirling round in space?
Is that a kindly face?

(The harsh voice of the FURY breaks the atmosphere)

FURY. You see, women enjoy being dominated and
humiliated...they enjoy being humiliated!

(The ghost-like atmosphere returns)

WOMAN. (repeating catatonically)
Who are those figures in white?...
are they the angels of light
or are they spiders on the wall,
about to fall on me?
Is that a table or a chair?
Is it there?
Or are they atoms whirling
round in space...

(From her kneeling position she looks up startled,
staring into the face of the MAN)

...is that a kindly face?

(The WOMAN, the MAN and the FURIES freeze into
a tableau. The FURIES' faces are gargoyle heads -
eyes bulging, tongues protruding.

Tape - the eerie voice of a WOMAN)

A WOMAN. (tape) Out of the daze - out of the memory
tracing. How much time has been lost. Light stars
have been flashing their messages across the skies.
And I've been left with the amoeba...

(The WOMAN's face is strained and anxious - as she
listens to the chanting voice.

Tape continues)

...it has taken a very long time for me to drag my
amorphous slug-body out of the mud. During the time I
have been unconscious...liver-drowsy...I have felt
this vaguely unsettles feeling above my head, as though
voices had been arguing my chances of awakening.

(Projected - questions to women. Black letters on
white screen.

1) Do you believe in penis envy?

2) Are you one of the great mass of women exploited
as cheap labour?

3) Does your sense of status or pride come from the man you live with rather than your own projects?

4) Do you think there is a <u>natural</u> role for woman?

5) Do you think motherhood is a mystical experience?

6) Can woman be other than isolated and trapped within the structure of the family?

7) Are you frightened of male ridicule and derision?

8) Would you define submitting to the will of others as an illness?

WOMAN's attention fixed to the screen.

The GROUP inches into life.

The MAN flicks a little dust from his lapel and casually begins his lecture. The questions disappear)

MAN. Now where were we? - we cannot have muddles - ah, yes, - a clear line for the universe is essential. Now, he who is a cat and wishes to be a dog - is in for trouble - and she who tries to wag a tail she does not possess is on a false wicket. The washing-up is a greasy business when it loses its mystical overtones; separated from its cultural meaning, it is nothing but a pile of dirty dishes. Prisons have to be inhabited by someone otherwise why build them? If the basket tries to walk away, where will the dog lie down?

(Projection of Rene Magritte slide of faceless man looking into mirror.

Exhausted the WOMAN struggles to answer)

WOMAN.
He who feels his feet
are planted firmly on the ground
must surely know
the ground is going round and round.

20

(Projections of mediaeval etchings, Durer, Hieronymous Bosch, etc.

GROUP begins to sing)

GROUP.
He who feels he's really sound of mind
Must surely know we're blind
The birds are singing - in a thing
We call - a sky
Above our heads
With which we think - we think.
A camera is working in a thing
- We call an eye
Where waterfalls
We call it - cry
Our hearts are beating
We call it love or fear
We think it's clear
Take a step - outside your skin
And begin
We may be so easily
A twist
In a dark sharp brain
Born of a scream
Cold as steel
That may be real
And it may become plain that it's mad to be sane.

(At the end of the song there is absolute quiet.

The face of the WOMAN brilliantly lit - possessed)

WOMAN. ...and it may become plain that it's mad to be sane.

(Sound of tolling bell)

WOMAN'S VOICE. (distant - remote - on tape)
The house is there
My face is pressed against the window
Menopausal - cheated - ridiculous
Envious - vindictive.

(Projection of Black Magic slides and stained-glass windows.

FURIES kneel in a religious group around the WOMAN. Two male FURIES hold candles.

The WOMAN kneels in the centre of the FURIES and leads them in prayer)

WOMAN & FURIES.
  'Hail Mary, full of grace etc.,'
  'Our Father which art in Heaven etc.,'

(The MAN laughs mockingly)

MAN. I thought so - if it's not sex, it's religion!

(The MAN walks forward and encircles the group as a Black Magic initiate and begins his wild incantation)

MAN.
  Cross on the door
  Leper in the pit
  Splinter in the soul
  Blood in the cave - order!

  Ant in the eye
  Knife in the brain - order!

  Cross in the heart
  Ice in the fire

(In the background the Christian chanting continues.

The MAN stretches out his hand and takes an imaginary chalice from a male FURY. He pretends to piss in it. He raises it up to the audience and drinks the imaginary urine in one gulp. He returns the imaginary chalice to the FURY)

MAN.
  Blood is the waves
  Splinter in the soul.

(The MAN's mockery turns to viciousness)

There's boil and bubble in my vein
Flea and maggot in my brain
Panic in my palms - and in my heart, there's hunger.

There are wasps and bees buzzing in my skull.

(The MAN stands beside the WOMAN facing the
audience. He mockingly satirises the marriage
service)

(Chanting)
With this ring I thee wed,
With this body I thee worship.

With all my worldly goods I thee endow.

(The MAN thrusts his genitals into the face of the
kneeling WOMAN)

Cry and clamour in my ears.
And from the corner of my eye
I perceive the cup is dry
And the bowl is empty.

(Piano begins slow wedding march)

WOMAN.
And there's nothing for my hunger.
Where was I at the crisis?

(The MAN stretches out his hand and helps her to her
feet.

They stand as bride and groom facing the audience.

The FURIES form a church arch.

The MAN whispers into her ear as the tender groom)

MAN. Down in the cave with the blood-stained sheets.

WOMAN. (flatly) Where is my history?

24

MAN. (mockingly) Paranoia.

WOMAN. Where was I when the battle was on?

(Over her face dawns the realisation of her fate.

The strains of the wedding march continue)

Once I had a thought of my very own.
I held it very frightened in the dark.
But she perceived it
Her eyes grew red.
She held her hand over my mouth
'till the thought was dead.
And she said

If you speak your bed will be cold –
'till you're old
You were born to cheat
And to keep your feet neat
Eyes not to see - but to shine
Lips not to reveal - but to taste like wine.
Use your fires - to burn another.
So I was taught for fourteen years by my mother.

(The MAN slides an imaginary wedding ring on the
WOMAN's finger.

The wedding march stops.

Popping of flashbulbs as the couple pose for photographs.

The MAN narcissistically preens himself - brushing
the lapels of his suit.

The FURIES rise as guests and the MAN joins them
seeking their approval. They shake his hand and each
others' in self-congratulation.

The WOMAN, isolated and alone, wanders towards the
audience for reassurance.

The GROUP begin the introduction to the song "Daddy's
Girl".

The **WOMAN** speaks the lines of "Daddy's Girl" in pleading tones musically reprised by the GROUP.

Projection of shop window dummies in bridal clothes)

WOMAN.
    Daddy's girl

SINGER.
    Daddy's girl - run away.

WOMAN.
    Run away.

SINGER.
    Daddy's girl -

WOMAN.
    Daddy's girl - <u>leave your house.</u>

SINGER.
    Fix your eye upon a star.

WOMAN.
    Fix your eye upon a star.

SINGER.
    Before they tell you

WOMAN.)
SINGER.) (together)
    <u>WHO</u> <u>YOU</u> <u>ARE</u>

WOMAN.
    When they sit you

SINGER.
    When they sit you - on their knee.

WOMAN.
    Stroke your thighs - and fix your curls.

SINGER.)
WOMAN.) (together)
    BEWARE MY DARLING
    GUARD YOUR LIFE

WOMAN.
    That's the game

SINGER.
    That's the game -
    They're going to play.

WOMAN.
    They are going to play.

SINGER.
    And in your Christmas stocking

WOMAN.
    Is the price - you're going to pay

SINGER.
    Break your dollies.

    (The WOMAN becomes more militant and assured)

WOMAN.
    Break your dollies
    Burn their dresses
    And the house you keep them in.
    The little apron with the hearts on.
    Little iron that works like real
    And the little plastic tea-set

SINGER.)
WOMAN.) (together)
    These are toys that
    GRIP LIKE STEEL.

    (The MAN raises his hand and halts the WOMAN. The
    FURIES step forward and face the audience)

MAN. Are you hostile, insecure - anxious, or just frankly
    unhappy?

Then eat babies - they're younger, softer and easier
to digest!

End of commercial break.

(He laughs maliciously and turns away.

The GROUP and the WOMAN continue "Daddy's Girl".

WOMAN.
Daddy's girl -

SINGER.
Daddy's girl

(The WOMAN stretches out her arms to an imaginary
child in the audience)

WOMAN.
So soon my darling
They'll have a bow around your neck
Tottering on your hind legs
Daddy's little pet.

SINGER.
They will teach you

SINGER.)
WOMAN.) (together)
How to whimper.
Wiles and guiles
How to please
How to cringe
How to simper...
And to stay...

WOMAN. (bitterly)
Down on your knees

SINGER.
Daddy's girl run away

WOMAN.
Daddy's girl - leave your house.

SINGER.) (together)
WOMAN.)
    Fix your eye upon a star.

WOMAN.
    Before they tell you

SINGER.
    Before they tell you

WOMAN.
    <u>WHO</u> <u>YOU</u> <u>ARE</u>

       (During "Daddy's Girl" the FURIES sit with arms
       around each other swaying behind the WOMAN.

       Projection of large telephone.

       Sound of telephone ringing.

       The MAN and the WOMAN go to opposite sides of the
       stage.

       The MAN mimes the lifting of a telephone receiver
       and dialling.

       The WOMAN mimes the lifting of her receiver.

       The FURIES watch expectantly)

MAN. Is that you?

       (The FURIES murmur together identifying with the
       moment)

       Are you a well, Madam - a well where a man can
       drink?

WOMAN. I'm not a feeding-bag if that's what you mean!

MAN. Is your home a place where a lion's wounds can be
    licked?

WOMAN. Did you say <u>boots</u>?

MAN. Ah! I can see you have an aggressive and antagonistic personality.

(The MAN drops his sophistication and breaks into obscenities)

I'm going to come over there and take your knickers down...

(Improvised obscenities from the MAN.

The projection of telephone grows larger. The light on the man recedes. Sound of heavy breathing mixed with the continual sound of dialling, interwoven with pathological obscenities.

As this happens one of the FURIES begins to masturbate and as the MAN reaches a crescendo of verbal obscenities, the FURY mimes a physical climax.

Light on the WOMAN's paralysed face)

WOMAN. (scream) HELP!

(The noise stops. Telephone vanishes)

MAN. May I remind you, Madam, that man's potency depends on constant affirmation from his wife.

WOMAN. (indignantly) What about my potency?

MAN. (laughing) Your potency! Your potency!

(The FURIES pick up the laughter among themselves)

(Arrogantly) May I remind you, Madam, that God is a man?

(The MAN leaves the telephone and takes up a position with a music sheet - as a portly baritone.

The GROUP begin pseudo-oratorio music for "God is a man".

Projection of mediaeval painting of 'Tired Jesus'.

The FURIES stand as in a church pew.

One female FURY sings a counter melody with the
MAN with operatic virtuosity)

God is a man
And that's how things began
Solemnly, with dignity
according to a plan
With Logic, not with magic,
That's how things began.
First the land and then the sea
How could that be done by a she?
Yes, God is an absolute
And the absolute is
Absolutely - He

The Master Plan
The Heavenly Scheme
Couldn't be a girlish dream
It took a lot of might
    To make the light
It took a lot of power
    To make a flower
And when out of the void - came
The Word
It is disgusting and absurd
To think those holy tones were thrown
In anything but a deep male baritone
God is a man, a man, a man,
And that's how things began.

("God is a man" finishes on crashing chords)

WOMAN. (timidly)
All things bright and beautiful...

(The MAN waves to the WOMAN from the opposite
side of the stage)

MAN. (coyly) It's me.

WOMAN. I know.

MAN. It's me.

> (For a moment they stand and look at each other as objects. They advance towards one another, machine-like, in abstract examination of the other.
>
> The FURIES begin to examine themselves and each other as if they were large inquisitive apes.
>
> The MAN repeats his boyish handwave)

> It's me.

> (The GROUP begin rhythmic enquiring music to the following dialogue.
>
> Projections of inward and outward movements of liquids in rhythm with the words and music. Slides of the MAN and the WOMAN with different and surprised enigmatic expressions.
>
> The MAN looks at his hands - and then into the WOMAN's eyes)

> It's me - I recognise myself - look at those eyes - ears - nose - ears set close together - each side of the head - one higher than the other - hands curled inwards; - I could never get my fingers to unfurl - not totally.

> (They inspect parts of each other's anatomy with awe and amazement)

WOMAN. (curiously) Who?

MAN. (flatly) Me.

> (Film projection of X-rays of moving human bodies)

WOMAN. Who? - it's me - I know who I am - I have examined myself carefully - in the bath - many times - in the mirror.

(They turn - looking to the audience for recognition)

MAN. We all have shaved - seen those clumps of hair clustered together in an undeniable shape - totally our own.

WOMAN. We all have glanced sideways in a shop window and known the shape - known it utterly - as it springs to greet us.

(The pace of the words grows faster, wilder. The couple encircle one another as strange animals)

MAN. The little finger that stands very slightly away from the others - length and breadth - size and shape - a tuft of hair that stands on end.

WOMAN. Feel of fat and tissue - line and gesture - dimension and proportion.

(More staccato - more incision - taut - strained - together)

MAN. That certain mistake in the anatomy - the image of ourselves.

WOMAN. Betrayed by the double chin - pigeon toes.

MAN. Hump - slump in the shoulders.

WOMAN. The mole that has extended itself.

MAN. The ingrained lines of the palm.

WOMAN. The position of the thumbs.

MAN. Constriction of the jaw.

WOMAN. Curve at the base of the spine.

TOGETHER. And finally emerging from the mixture - ourselves - we cannot be mistaken - it is me - it is me - it is me.

(They try to drown out the <u>other</u> - who insists over and over, <u>me</u> - <u>me</u> - me.

The GROUP breaks the words with staccato music.
The couple join the GROUP's sound <u>insistently</u>)

MAN.
　　<u>Forced</u> to be the aggressor
　　<u>Forced</u> to be the oppressor
　　<u>Forced</u> to take it on the chin.

WOMAN.
　　Forced to be the appeaser
　　Forced to be the pleaser
　　Lie down.

MAN.
　　Stand up.

TOGETHER.
　　Give in
　　the roles are set
　　We dare not falter
　　the rules are there
　　we cannot alter.

WOMAN. Children must be nourished.

MAN. Bread must be won.

TOGETHER. Before our living has really begun.

MAN. She's my <u>wife</u>.

WOMAN. I'm not his <u>mother</u>.

MAN. She's my <u>wife.</u>

WOMAN. Where is my lover?

MAN. We said that we would love.

WOMAN. It's a joke.

34

MAN. What I wanted was a helpmate not a yoke.

TOGETHER. Are we forced to play these roles for life?

MAN. Husband.

WOMAN. And wife. (Tremulously) I show my fear in the
night.

MAN. (terrified) My shaving mirror sees my fright.

WOMAN. (with growing horror) He doesn't really see me.

MAN. She doesn't know who I am - who am I? She doesn't
know who I am.

WOMAN. Who am I?

MAN. She doesn't know who I am?

WOMAN. Who am I?

> (The voice of a FAIRGROUND BARKER (on tape)
> stops the couple dead - frozen to their spots)

BARKER. Your lucky colour is blue. Your lucky number
four.

> (The MAN and WOMAN rush frantically about straining
> their heads towards the voice)

> Your star is shooting high.

MAN. (excitedly) Yes, yes!

BARKER. Tomorrow a windfall.

MAN. (very excited) A windfall - did you hear that? - a
windfall!

WOMAN. (frantically) What about me?

BARKER. (voice on megaphone) Keep fresh. Violets are
blue.

36

WOMAN. (desperately) What about the lonely nerves?

(The couple listen breathlessly for their future.

Sound of radio crackle and the radio goes dead)

MAN. (anxiously) A windfall - did you hear that?

(Soft refrain on the guitar as the MAN speaks - sad - nostalgic - full of yearning. His eyes look up to the stars)

- a windfall - my fortune was about to be revealed - not snow crystals - in sight or dark psychic eyes - you know, Margaret - have I not laughed at dream fragments - splinter pictures - corner eye shadows - flicker-dark movies - have I ever sat with you and compiled histories from down under the blankets - no - I'm a solid man - dealing with precariousness - could I afford - could I balance the books if I gave a definition to every little brain quirk - I'm working on the assumption that the system can be saved.

(End of guitar refrain)

MAN. (frantically)
The system can be saved!
The system can be saved!
The system can be saved!

(His face contorts - he clenches his hands and begins to list his anxieties as though he's chasing a rat in his brain)

If I sell this one - and buy another, the profits could pay for - if I ask the bank - and the bank allows it... I could hold out 'till the 6th. - no, the 6th. would be too late... the 5th.... if I could stall the other owners...
(Improvised...dozens of fragmented thoughts...a maze of worries)

(A few moments after the MAN begins his list of worries, the WOMAN in the opposite corner of the

stage begins to list hers - the couple totally
oblivious of one another.

The FURIES stealthily creep away, hands over ears,
and sit in a line, facing the back theatre wall)

WOMAN. Fetch the laundry - collect the children - dog to
the vet, spring-clean the bedroom - iron the curtains -
visit the hairdresser - 'phone my mother - feed the
goldfish - remove the stains - clean the cupboards...
(Improvise a seemingly endless list of tasks - that
stretch on - and on - covering her whole life)

(The FURIES count on their fingers, and add and
subtract invisible arithmetic on the floor. Others
scratch their heads in complete bewilderment.

During this sequence the theatre is dark except for
light on the couples' tormented faces.

Sound of a frog croaking - then a jackal screeching -
followed by a rush of wind.

These primitive sounds build, creating a primeval
forest and ending in a volcanic eruption.

Then there is silence.

And the couple turn to look at the screen on the back
wall.

Black and white news film. A man is standing on the
parapet of a sky-scraper. He clutches the railings
and looks down at the street. Spectators wait below.
He hesitates - then he jumps. His body hits the ground
- Police rush forward. REPEAT SEQUENCE. The
FURIES stand in line looking up at the screen -
reaching out as though to catch the falling man. They
moan each time he hits the ground. The sound of a
train passing.

The MAN and the WOMAN are still seated at the front
of the stage.

Cut to absolute silence and blackness in the theatre.

A Golden Buddha fills the environment. A golden light floods the stage. The sound of soft Tantra music. The FURIES seat themselves in Yoga positions, and begin a Tantra chant.

(On tape) FEMALE VOICE slowly chanting. Tantra chanting continues softly behind the poem)

VOICE.
    I think that you think - a worm
    that a fly
    mirror-crushed - blood eagled
    spread on an exaggerated pin
    could sweat out the issue
    I think that she thinks -
    She drips with pain
    I think I think
    we must examine her again
    now - I think that she thinks
    that I think she'll die
    that she'll ooze out perpetually
    on my sleeve
    contriving to catch me
    in her bulbous eye
    but I think that she thinks
    that I think she cheats me
    allowing her dainty furry
    shiver-leg
    to run down the glass and kiss me.

(A succession of Buddhas and Tantric art.

The GROUP begin the Song "So wise so fair")

GROUP.
    I see you in a far far place
        A million years - darling one
    A sound in space, spinning on your lips
        Burning on a distant sun
        Limpid eyes - golden hair
    SO WISE, SO FAIR

A million years to hold my darling
    You'll never know the words I've said
Can I hold you my beloved
    You'll be born when I am dead
    All the princes icy-cold
    In the tomb of my despair
SO WISE, SO FAIR
You are drifting on a star
    Watching all my selfish pain
You are drifting on a star
    Loving me in vain
A million years and you'll be born
    Wise and free and full of grace
    Without the need - without the want
    With love reflected in your face
SO WISE, SO FAIR.

(At the end of the song the atmosphere changes
abruptly.

The GROUP begin bouncing happy holiday music.

Projections of gaudy holiday slides: beaches,
umbrellas, cafes etc.

The FURIES leap and shout the names of holiday
resorts: Alicante! Torremolinos! Corfu!

Two male FURIES (as waiters) each bring a chair
and put them together in the centre of the stage.

The MAN and the WOMAN sit at the cafe table.

The MAN tips one of the male FURIES.

The FURIES sit in a semi-circle behind the couple as
other holiday-makers, sunbathing.

The MAN and the WOMAN are tense, obviously in the
middle of a row.

Guitar music begins suggesting a nervous strained
atmosphere.

40

As the couple begin their dialogue, the guitar echoes
their jangled nerves.

The music rises and falls as the argument assumes
different levels - reaching a crescendo as the row
explodes.

The WOMAN is tearful and self pitying)

WOMAN. Perhaps you'd rather be with someone else.

(The MAN is embarrassed and hostile)

MAN. Another time, another place.

WOMAN. (bitterly) Another face?

(Pause. Tense silence. The WOMAN sighs)

MAN. Perhaps you'd rather sit here on your own, <u>alone</u>.

(She gets up from her chair, as though to leave)

WOMAN. I'll go home.

MAN. <u>Sit down</u> - and stop expecting - stop <u>demanding</u>.

(The WOMAN sits reluctantly.

A moment's silence)

WOMAN. Don't forget your pill.

(The MAN clenches his teeth)

MAN. Stop <u>insisting</u>.

WOMAN. That I'm a person too - and not just you.

(Silence. Irritation is mounting. The voices become
more hectic. The guitar more grating)

Perhaps you need me just to fill a space - because you
doubt that you <u>exist</u>.

41

MAN. Must you persist - explaining every minute who I
am - I'm just a man.

(The mood is more out of control)

WOMAN. (fast pace with suppressed tears) Perhaps you
think I ought to like the fact - you have to prove it
five times a day with every whore you meet - on
every street.

MAN. We're in a public place - don't make a scene.

WOMAN. If I want to scream - I'll scream.

(Guitar crashes to a halt.

She screams and then there is a silence)

(With quiet self-control)
Don't forget your pill.
Ask him for the bill.

MAN. Perhaps you'd like to write me out a chart - to
learn by heart, to learn by rote.

WOMAN. You're immature and cold and afraid of growing
old.

MAN. Stop trying to tell me who I am - I'm just a man -
who'd like some peace.

WOMAN. A piece of what? - a piece of skirt - a piece of
cake - without the fee that life demands.

MAN. Stop trying to tell me who I am - I'm just a man.

(The WOMAN gets up from her chair as though to leave,
but the MAN stretches out his hand and halts her. He
smiles at her lovingly and coaxes her down onto his
knee. He presses her head down into his neck, stroking
her hair and whispering words of comfort.

Suddenly he grabs her hair, and pulls her head round
sharply to face the audience. Her face is wooden and

smiling - eyes round and rolling, mouth a plastic chattering slit.

She is the ventriloquist's dummy.

Black theatre but for a large strong spot on the couple for the 'Cabaret act'.

The FURIES clap and wait expectantly for the 'act'.

(Very slow and ingratiating) Now, what were we learning about yesterday, Ethel?

ETHEL. (anxiously) I don't remember, Victor.

VICTOR. (slowly and soothingly) Yes, you do Ethel - we were learning about - (Pause) femininity.

(The dummy, ETHEL, pauses for a second trying to comprehend the word - then she breaks up the word as a child who does not understand)

ETHEL. Fem - in - in - ity!

VICTOR. (pleased) Good! Now what does the word femininity mean, Ethel?

ETHEL. (very fast through clacking teeth) A traitor? A sucker? A sap?

(Loud roars of dummy laughter from ETHEL. Pause)

VICTOR. (with slow suppressed irritation) No Ethel. Femininity means (He lingers, savouring the phrase) a femme du monde (Pause) a lady of charm... and what does a lady of charm do, Ethel?

ETHEL. (swiftly) Lie through her fucking teeth.

(Raucous laughter from the DUMMY.

VICTOR turns ETHEL over his knee and smacks her bottom - then he sits her upright, recovers his composure, and begins again)

43

VICTOR. Now you're a very naughty girl, Ethel. A very
     naughty girl.

ETHEL. (subdued) Sorry, Victor!

VICTOR. And you haven't learned your lesson, Ethel.

ETHEL. No Victor!

VICTOR. Never mind. I'm going to take you to a cocktail
     party.

ETHEL. (thrilled) To a cocktail party!

VICTOR. Right - now - you go to this cocktail party.

ETHEL. (slowly) I'm going to this cocktail party.

VICTOR. Right - and you meet a man.

ETHEL. (narrow-eyed) What kind of a man, Victor?

VICTOR. (irritably) Just a man.

ETHEL. O.K., O.K., don't be cross, Victor.

VICTOR. Now - where was I?...

ETHEL. I was meeting this man.

VICTOR. Now Ethel, listen carefully - this man puts his
     wet greasy hand on your shoulder - what do you do?

ETHEL. (swiftly) Smack him in the kisser!

     (She roars with dummy laughter)

VICTOR. (very angry) No, no, no!

ETHEL. (sheepishly) Sorry Victor, it just popped out.

VICTOR. Yes, but why was it a wrong answer?

ETHEL. (in dummy confusion) I don't know, Victor.

44

VICTOR. (coaxing) Because if you insult this nice man, Ethel...

ETHEL. (parrot-like) If I insult this man –

VICTOR. (deliberately) He'll lose his confidence...

ETHEL. (brainwashed) And I'll fracture his ego!

VICTOR. (slowly) And he won't be able to go out in the world.

ETHEL. And build a little house (With appalled realisation of what this implies) where he can put his wet greasy hand on me anytime he wishes!

(The MAN throws the ventriloquist's DUMMY into her chair where she remains doll-like throughout his next act. The MAN taps across the stage in the manner of a third-rate variety comic.

One brilliant spot on MAN. He moves towards the audience smiling ingratiatingly.

MAN as comic (Patting hat – lighting cigarette). Lewd wink and eye roll at woman in the audience.

The 'act' begins.

Each sentence has the rhythm and intonation of comic patter, but the actual words are either swallowed or fractured and their exact meaning is not decipherable. Only the repressed sexiness and fetishistic gestures suggest the exact assault of the final word of each phrase. The loose mouth that lolls around the garbled phrase tightens into mechanical precision when he spits out the operative word. The word which is the butt of the joke impacted with contempt and derision.

The act is punctuated by the drum)

MAN. (as comic) Well...er...well...my wife.

(Loud canned laughter and wild laughter from the

45

FURIES)

MAN. (as COMIC) And...er...er... (Pause) her bloody
    knickers -

(Canned laughter and applause)

And er like...er...her....bloody hormones...er...
er...fucking time of month...

(Canned laughter more hysterical)

...er...er...bloody women drivers...er bloody
women bosses...well...er...bloody lesbians...er
well my bloody mother-in-law...and...er...er...
nagging bitches...

(Canned laughter reaches climax and cuts out suddenly.

The manner of COMIC changes abruptly to a sophisticated
French mimist. Soft piano music begins.

The MAN very smooth - slow - insidious - with his
hands outlines the shape of a voluptuous female body.

He starts to undress this imaginary form.

He plucks the nipples, squeezes the breasts, touches
the cunt.

He defines this creature as an object.

A mime describing his contempt of the female species.

As each indignity is brought to bear - he pauses
suggestively, colluding with the audience through sly
winks and furtive gestures.

The moment is reached when he is about to assault the
figure he has created.

He breaks the mood - and re-enters the character of the
vulgar joker.

The piano music stops. Drum roll)

MAN. (as comic) Well, all things aside...as I was saying - my wife - her bloody mother-in-law - their knickers - their tampax...their fucking tits.

(The MAN suddenly begins to lose his laughter to reveal a monstrous hostility. He takes an imaginary knife from his pocket. He bends over this invented female body and begins to hack - as though he is dismembering it.)

(Frantically) My mother - her breasts - and her cunt.

(He hacks murderously with the imaginary knife)

My mother
My fucking mother
I'm cutting up my fucking mother.

(He drops the knife from his hand and kneels, horrified by his efforts.

He begins to whimper - a guilty two-year-old)

Mummy, mummy, I love you mummy.

(The MAN convulses on the floor in an infantile rage.

Spot on the WOMAN on the chair who metamorphoses into the omnipotent mother-goddess.

She rises and looks down at her body, smiling admiringly at its contours)

WOMAN. Defined as something unique.

(The GROUP begin slow hypnotic music.

The female SINGER stretches out her arms as a prophetic mermaid.

The theatre is filled with rich, pulsating colours)

SINGER. But never quite whole.

WOMAN. (narcissistically) But with special qualities.

(The GROUP echo the WOMAN's words with inhuman, cavelike, primitive sounds)

SINGER. But not the ones that matter.

WOMAN. I'm an angel, a flower, a bird.

(She begins to sway in a mermaid dance as if under hypnosis)

SINGER. (spitting an omen) When you die you'll be shit - to fertilize plant life.

(The WOMAN purses her lips coyly, thrusting out nymphet breasts)

WOMAN. But they tell me the sex struggle's over - that it is all out of date - that there isn't any hate.

SINGER. (violently) I say it's a cauldron - bubbling - fuming and waiting to spill.

(Projections of witchcraft images.

The music becomes slow and possessed)

She's got witchcraft in her thighs.

WOMAN. I've got witchcraft...

(The WOMAN slowly peels off her black jacket - drugged with her own desirability)

SINGER. She's got witchcraft and a magic art. And they promise her that one day - she will be released from the stone.

(The WOMAN stretches out her arms longingly)

WOMAN. One day there'll be something of my own.

(The SINGER points at the WOMAN ominously - her

voice harshens and breaks)

SINGER.
    Meanwhile, Goddess, pray
    meanwhile, Goddess, watch the sailors on the ships
    And wear your garment of <u>non-exist</u>.

    (Sound of the crashing sea.

    The WOMAN lets down her hair and shakes it,
    seductively)

WOMAN. Look into my eyes.

SINGER. She cannot see. Her eyes are mares' eyes and
    vixens' and cows' eyes.

    (The WOMAN enclosing herself in her arms in a
    gesture of self-love)

WOMAN. My love says wait for the time when I shall be
    released from the stone. And there'll be something
    to call my own.

    (The WOMAN unbuttons her blouse.

    The music changes abruptly from hypnotic trance to
    brash burlesque.

    The projections dance their violent sexual colours and
    shapes - crimson and purple.

    The WOMAN becomes strident and fetishist and begins
    to strip.

    The MAN is still huddled on the floor cursing her in
    soft whispers 'till he is silenced by her powers.

    The WOMAN begins her strip-tease, removing another
    piece of clothing at each stanza. Throaty and brash - she
    is a parody of the Bar-room Lily - slow, husky,
    drawling voice - eyeing the males with crude seduc-
    tiveness.

The words are spoken rhythmically supported by the
heavy throbbing music)

She has pearls of wisdom from the deep
A six star prism
And a comb of molten gold
She has a toad that trembles to her touch
She has crystal baubles - where your future's told
And liquid lead - running from her crutch
She has music - so whistle in the dark
It's heard only by the grey wolf on the hill
She's got poison - to lace your drink at night
When she's bent you to her - four plus will
She's got honey - to spread upon your bread
She's got waterfalls - to trickle down your heart
So - crunch my love
Find all the bees are dead
She knew that you were dead - right from the start.

(The WOMAN throws away her last piece of clothing,
her panties, into the whistling, cheering FURIES.
She is naked and, suddenly realising her vulnerable
state, she backs away towards the wall)

But in my sleep I hear a voice groan
I hear a strangled foetus voice groan.

(The SINGER distorts herself into an ancient hag - and
points a crooked finger)

SINGER.
    She hears a strangled foetus voice g-r-o-a-n
    Nothing of your own.

    (Projection of cathedral stained-glass window which
    falls from the back wall, covering the naked WOMAN
    in its brilliant patterns

    She falls to her knees.

    The FURIES rise as a derisive night-club audience,
    booing and hissing. They move towards the back wall
    of the theatre removing all their clothes, flinging them
    at the naked WOMAN.

They move towards her, and lift her, raising her knees into the birth position.

Two of the FURIES draw a sheet of white plastic from between her legs, forming a screen in front of the WOMAN at the edge of the stage.

Projection on small screen: close-up of a vagina.

Large projection on back wall of the rest of the naked WOMAN in labour.

Sound of birth from FURIES and on tape.

Agonised breathing from WOMAN in labour.

From behind the small screen, a head of one of the FURIES emerges tearing the screen in the centre of the vagina.

One by one the FURIES crawl through the hole groaning and wailing as new-born babes, tumbling onto the floor in foetal positions.

Several of the FURIES fall forward into the laps of the first row, they cling terrified to members of the audience wailing and shrieking, "Mummy! Mummy! Mummy!"

The two female FURIES who are holding the screen collapse with birth pangs.

The tableau is arrested by the sound of a ROBOT on tape. Cybernetic film sequence)

ROBOT. Who is responsible for this evolutionary mistake?

(The FURIES encircle the WOMAN, kneeling around her, pointing their fingers at her accusingly)

FURIES. She! She! She! She!

(Tapes running backwards.

The MAN steps out of the shadows and views the
GROUP coolly, scientifically, and addresses the
audience.

MAN. You see the individual may achieve a false fusion
of the aggressive and the sexual, by converting this
aggression into masochism - but for this to occur there
must be a reliable persecutor - and a reliable
persecutor is always a sadistic lover - a sadistic
lover...Isn't it envy? Penis envy? The absent organ in
the public lavatory.

ROBOT. Schizophrenics are the result of basic alienation
with the mother.

(The WOMAN rises from the group and lets out a wild
scream of frustration)

WOMAN'S VOICE. (on tape) Victim submits to the will of
others.

ROBOT. (on tape) The natural role for woman is the
submissive one.

(She runs to the back wall of the theatre.

Projection of an enormous gas oven with an open door.

Screams of babies are heard.

A hag wildly laughing on tape)

HAG. The uterus is the great divider.

(The WOMAN leans motionless against the open oven)

ROBOT. (on tape) We are talking about madness.

WOMAN'S VOICE. (on tape - very faint) Dreams are
political.

(Sound of gas escaping.

Whispered words - almost a lullaby -)

WOMAN.
>Handle on the bag is breaking
>Last bone on the spine is aching.

>(Deafening noise of aircraft overhead)

>White walls
>White chenille
>Pale wood and eau de Nille.

GROUP.
>Thin walls - grey sky
>A charcoal bird etched on the eye.

>Baby's in his strip pine crib
>Dribbling on his plastic bib.

>The latest film star's back from Rome
>I am in my little home.

>There's the gas oven Christian clean
>Brand X soap and spleen.

>Listen to the gas escaping
>Listen to the noise it's making.

>Listen to the building rumbling
>Listen to the foundations crumbling.

>(The WOMAN turns away from the oven and staggers
>towards the audience...

>Projection changes to an open gas oven now full of
>children's toys.

>The WOMAN is demented.

>Almost dark theatre. Projection of huge T.V. screen -
>talking heads - without sound - electronic hum)

WOMAN.
>The faces flicker on the box...
>They're analysing love
>Another lady fink

So neat about the feet
So reasonable with men
So personally dainty, self-controlled
- leaning slightly forward,
- sure to please
I suppose, she says - there is a slight
hormonal trap - for us - ...A little
kapo smile hovers on her lips...
I'm afraid your right - Birth - ah yes
Birth does separate us - I suppose inevitably -
from total human dignity -
How clever of you to see - I do agree.

(She has reached the edge of the stage - the schizo-
phrenic pleading for understanding)

I like to keep myself very clean, there's something
disgusting about dribble, something vile like bile.
Have you ever noticed dogs when they grow old? - how
they bumble and sway towards you - well, my mother...

(The WOMAN turns away from the audience and moves
towards the circle of FURIES, and collapses in their
centre.

They bend over her enclosing her as the petals of a
flower)

(Brokenly) Well, my mother...my mother...

(She sobs)

WOMAN'S VOICE. (on tape) What treatment can I have?
What doctor exists that does not demand my submission
as the price for peace?

(The MAN moves towards the group towering over the
prostrate WOMAN.

The WOMAN, sensing his presence, looks up suddenly)

WOMAN. (catatonically) Who are you?

MAN. I am the cooler.

(She puts her head on his arm pleadingly. He removes
it with disgust)

I am the third part of the three-handed con trick. There
is the softener, the taker and me - the cooler - you
have been taken - and I am here to see you don't belly-
ache to the authorities.

(He takes her arm and mimes giving her an injection.

Sound of thudding heart-beat)

WOMAN'S VOICE. (on tape) Relief floods through me as I
    allow his contempt - and we agree I'm mentally
    unstable.

    (The WOMAN watches the projection of a needle
    puncturing a vein.

    She begins to smile like a half crazed child)

MAN. (smoothly) I am here to ease your pain.

    (The MAN sits on a chair and reads the 'Times'.

    The FURIES scream like hungry babies.

    Frantically the WOMAN mimes the heating and filling
    of feeding bottles.

    The noise of the screaming FURIES grows louder as
    they clamour for their feeds.

    The WOMAN hands bottles around the yelling group,
    and as each one receives his feed, his screaming
    stops, replaced by the sound of sucking.

    The WOMAN, distraught, wanders around the sucking
    group, reciting brokenly to herself.

    Soft nursery piano music)

WOMAN.
    One little pink cup for me
    One little blue cup for him
    six o'clock - the bird has flown.
    Lovers are quiet
    the news is active and alive -
    even in war
    my milk has dried - the teats are sour
    the screams are regular
    four-hourly - on the hour
    the oven's waiting for a cake
    my head is still out.

    (A bell tolls)

    The young have promised me a tribe, an Indian
    house and a coloured mat
    beads to hang on my breasts
    now that they're flat
    serenity - traditional love -

SINGER. (softly) and even peace of mind.

    (The MAN folds his newspaper and puts it on the seat
    of his chair.

    He walks towards the WOMAN and helps her into a
    loose peignoir. He is reasonable - gentle - merciless)

MAN. Prisons have to be inhabited by someone, otherwise
    why build them?

    (The WOMAN smiles at the MAN happily. He takes her
    in his arms and they begin to waltz - the romantic
    couple.

    The GROUP begin to play)

GROUP.
    So pity the poor lady
    who from the age of four
    looked at the man with awe and trembled
    pity the poor lady
    from the age of three

perched there pretty - on papa's knee
looked into that hairy face -
and vowed
I must get one for me
search - search
for one who'd make her quiver
a master who'd dictate the terms
one who'd make her shiver
'cos he didn't like her hat
didn't like her chat
thought she said too much -
or too little
one that she could praise
concentrate her gaze
through a foggy haze -
of non-committal -
lovely moon - evening skies
<u>and lies</u> -

(The couple enact a little choreographed sketch of the
tender husband and the coy wife.

The MAN gets a mask and hides it behind his back
playfully, as a longed-for present.

She pleads to see it - he teases her - holding the
object out of reach.

Finally she wins and he takes the mask and puts it on
her face.

It is the mask of a wizened senile old woman.

The couple waltz. A spotlight follows them.

The GROUP continue to sing)

GROUP.
   ...fine, find - one that she could fear
up to scratch - toe the line
and not make it too clear
if she didn't like his touch
wouldn't be his crutch
thought his jokes too lewd

or too simple
one that she could coax
one that she could hoax
through those magic cloaks
of little dimples
lovely moon - evening skies
and lies

pity the poor lady
crazy with confusion
under the delusion
she's been swindled
it's out of date
to talk of rights
she's got the vote
who'd ask for more
she's got the key
to her own front door
it's her domain
to do the same
day by day
since time began
praise the man
and pity the poor lady -

(The couple stop at the edge of the stage.

A smiling young MAN. A grotesque old HAG.

The MAN touches the WOMAN under her chin and then
grins at the audience. He begins to laugh - the laughter
grows - 'till he convulses helplessly.

The FURIES laugh.

WOMAN'S VOICE. (on tape) The rage is still impacted
    within us - I am frightened of the on-coming explosion.

(The WOMAN pirouettes - alone - round and round the
stage - oblivious of the joke)

C AND B PLAYSCRIPTS

		Cloth	Paper
*PS 1	TOM PAINE by Paul Foster	21s	9s
PS 18	EARLY MORNING by Edward Bond	25s	9s
*PS 29	WELCOME TO DALLAS, MR. KENNEDY by Kaj Himmelstrup trans. Christine Hauch	25s	10s
PS 33	MACRUNE'S GUEVARA by John Spurling	25s	9s
PS 38	DISCOURSE ON VIETNAM by Peter Weiss trans. Geoffrey Skelton	38s	18s
*PS 39	! HEIMSKRINGLA ! or THE STONED ANGELS by Paul Foster	30s	12s
PS 43	THE NUNS by Eduardo Manet trans. Robert Baldick	25s	10s
PS 45	A MACBETH by Charles Marowitz	30s	12s
*PS 47	SAMSON and ALISON MARY FAGAN by David Selbourne	25s	12s
*PS 53	FOUR BLACK REVOLUTIONARY PLAYS (Experimental Death Unit 1, A Black Mass, Great Goodness of Life, Madheart) by Leroi Jones	25s	12s

*All plays marked thus are represented for dramatic
presentation by:
C and B (Theatre) Ltd, 18 Brewer Street London W1